George Catlin

Painter of Indian Life

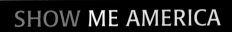
SHOW ME AMERICA

George Catlin

Painter of Indian Life

Richard Worth

Sf
Sharpe Focus
an imprint of M.E. Sharpe, Inc.

SERIES CONSULTANT
Jeffrey W. Allison
Paul Mellon Collection
Educator, Virginia Museum of Fine Arts

Cover Art:
Buffalo Bull's Back Fat, Head Chief, Blood Tribe. Blackfoot (George Catlin);
Buffalo Hunt Surround, no. 9, Lithograph (George Catlin).

Sharpe Focus
An imprint of M.E. Sharpe, Inc.
80 Business Park Drive
Armonk, NY 10504
www.sharpe-focus.com

Series created by Kid Graphica, LLC
Series designed by Gilda Hannah
Map: Mapping Specialists Limited

Library of Congress Cataloging-in-Publication Data

Worth, Richard.
George Catlin: painter of Indian life / Richard Worth.
  p. cm. — (Show me America)
Includes bibliographical references and index.
ISBN 978-0-7656-8152-2 (hardcover: alk. paper)
1. Catlin, George, 1796–1872—Juvenile literature. 2. Painters—United
States—Biography—Juvenile literature. 3. Indians in art—Juvenile
literature. 4. West (U.S.)—In art—Juvenile literature. I. Title.

ND237.C35W67 2008
759.13—dc22
[B]   2007040694

Printed in Malaysia

9 8 7 6 5 4 3 2 1

Contents

Two figures from *Drinks the Juice of the Stone, in Ball-Player's Dress. 1834. Choctaw. George Catlin*

George Catlin's Creed

I love the people who have always made me welcome to the best they had.

I love a people who are honest without laws, who have no jails and no poorhouses.

I love a people who keep the commandments without ever having read them or heard them preached from the pulpit.

I love a people who never swear, who never take the name of God in vain.

I love a people "who love their neighbors as they love themselves."

I love a people who worship God without a Bible, for I believe that God loves them also.

I love the people whose religion is all the same, and who are free from religious animosities.

I love the people who have never raised a hand against me, or stolen my property, where there was no law to punish either.

I love the people who have never fought a battle with white men, except on their own ground.

I love and don't fear mankind where God has made and left them, for there they are children.

I love a people who live and keep what is their own without locks and keys.

I love all people who do the best they can. And oh, how I love a people who don't live for the love of money.

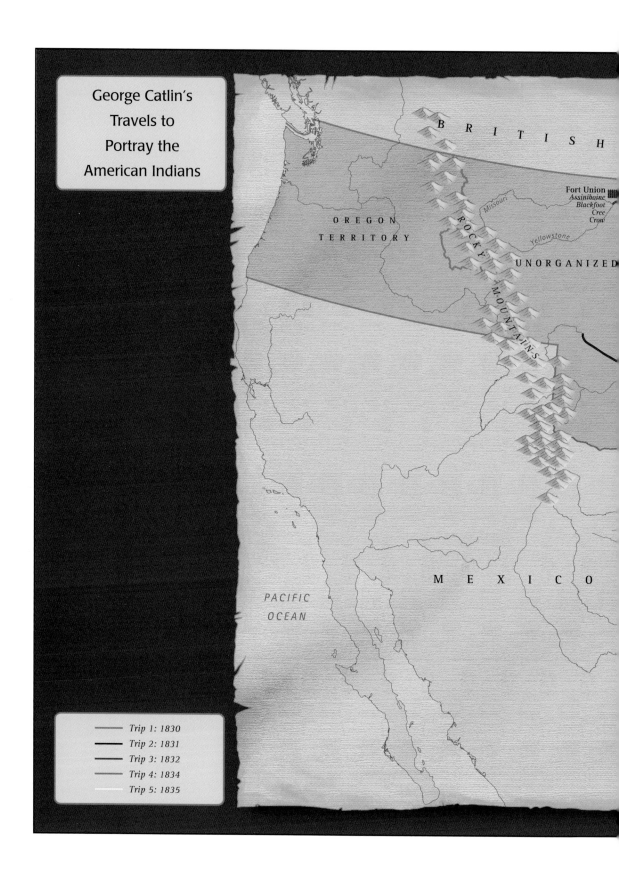

George Catlin's
Travels to
Portray the
American Indians

BRITISH

Fort Union
Assiniboine
Blackfoot
Cree
Crow

OREGON
TERRITORY

ROCKY MOUNTAINS

Missouri

Yellowstone

UNORGANIZED

MEXICO

PACIFIC
OCEAN

Trip 1: 1830
Trip 2: 1831
Trip 3: 1832
Trip 4: 1834
Trip 5: 1835

P O S S E S S I O N S

Clark
lan

TERRITORY

MICHIGAN

Fort Snelling
Siour
Chippewa

Prairie du Chien

Fort Crawford
Sauk and Fox

Camp Des Moines
Sauk and Fox

TERRITORY

re

Pawnee
naha
Oto

Fort
Leavenworth
Delaware
Iowa
Shawnee

ILLINOIS

INDIANA

OHIO

Litchfield

St. Louis

MISSOURI

KENTUCKY

TENNESSEE

Fort Gibson
Cherokee
Choctaw
Osage

ARKANSAS
TERRITORY

Cincinnati

NORTH CAROLINA

SOUTH
CAROLINA

MAINE

VERMONT NEW
HAMPSHIRE

NEW YORK

Albany

MASSACHUSSETTS

CONNECTICUT

Litchfield

Wilkes-Barre

New York

NEW
JERSEY

PENNSYLVANIA

Philadelphia

MARYLAND

DELAWARE

WASHINGTON, D.C.

VIRGINIA

ALABAMA

GEORGIA

MISSISSIPPI

ATLANTIC
OCEAN

LOUISIANA

New Orleans

FLORIDA TERRITORY

Map   **9**

This portrait of George Catlin as a young man was painted by the Philadelphia artist John Neagle.

CHAPTER ONE

Exhibit in New York City

The history and customs of such a people,
preserved by pictorial illustrations,
are themes worthy of the life-time of one man.
—*George Catlin*

In September 1837, an unusual exhibit opened in New York City. In fact, nothing like it had ever been seen in the United States. At first, only a few people came to the exhibition, which was held in Clinton Hall. But as word spread, the crowds grew larger. Eventually, 600 people packed into the hall on a single evening. And each person paid 50¢, a fairly large sum of money in those days.

New Yorkers had gathered to see the paintings of a little-known artist named George Catlin. Since 1830, the wiry forty-one-year-old Catlin had traveled among American Indian tribes living in the West. Carrying his paints and canvases, the artist had recorded the cultures of the forty-eight tribes that he had visited.

Catlin's portraits were breathtaking. They presented the proud people of the western Great Plains. Catlin had captured the timeless expressions of chiefs, medicine men, veteran warriors, and beautiful Indian women. They were clothed in long, flowing headdresses, finely decorated clothing made from animal skins, and a wide assortment of jewelry.

In addition to portraits, Catlin also had painted many scenes showing Indian customs. Some scenes showed the Plains warriors hunting buffalo, others presented native religious ceremonies, and still others were windows into tribal village life. In addition to displaying his paintings in the exhibit, Catlin also included many items

that he had collected on his journeys. There were Comanche war lances and a tepee from the Crow Indians, as well as drums, peace pipes, shields, spears, and tomahawks.

Each night during the exhibit, Catlin spoke enthusiastically about the Indian culture of the West. Many people regarded the Indians as savages. But Catlin had found that they treated him with great kindness and respect. And they always had dealt honestly with him. The artist went on to say that white men frequently had not treated the Indians in the same way.

Treaties had been made with the Indian tribes, only to be broken, Catlin said. White traders had used alcohol to take advantage of the Indians, purchasing large piles of precious beaver furs for as little as a single bottle of liquor. Soldiers also had brought deadly disease to the Indians.

Although some white people who saw the exhibit praised Catlin's work, others were openly skeptical. They did not believe all that the artist was telling them. Many regarded Indians as bloodthirsty savages, thieves, and murderers. They thought that the Native American lifestyle was far inferior to their own.

Catlin showed them his portrait of Keokuk (Kee-o-kuk), chief of the Sauk and Fox tribes, seated on a magnificent horse. Many people in the audience said that no Indian horse could be that beautiful. But in November, Kee-o-kuk himself appeared at the exhibit. Catlin asked the crowd "why Kee-o-kuk could not ride as good a horse as any white man." They had no answer.

Catlin praised the simplicity of a people who were not primarily interested in material possessions. But he also presented a dark side of the Indian way of life. One of

Opposite: "The head chief of the Black Feet Nation," Catlin wrote, "is a good looking and dignified Indian, about fifty years of age, and superbly dressed."

Kee-o-kuk on Horseback. Sauk and Fox. George Catlin, 1835

The chief of the Sauk and Fox tribes, Kee-o-kuk, and his followers did not oppose the advance of whites. They moved first west of the Mississippi and then to a reservation in Kansas. Kee-o-kuk died there in 1848.

these was a ceremony called O-kee-pa, practiced by the Mandan tribe. In this ritual, boys were initiated into manhood through brutal torture. When audiences saw Catlin's pictures of the O-kee-pa ceremony, they doubted what the artist was showing them. Although he had certificates from witnesses to prove what he had seen, Catlin was harshly questioned by many observers. They simply did not believe him.

These mixed reactions to George Catlin, his striking paintings, and his controversial opinions would follow him throughout his career. But he never wavered in his courageous commitment to present the true story of the Plains Indians. Catlin was among the first Americans to dedicate themselves to such a mission—to record a unique way of life before it disappeared.

Interior View of the Medicine Lodge, Mandan O-kee-pa Ceremony. George Catlin, 1832

Catlin painted the medicine lodge where the brutal coming-of-age ritual called O-kee-pa was held. The young men's survival of the ordeal was proof that they were protected by the Great Spirit. "My heart has sickened with disgust for so abominable and ignorant a custom," wrote Catlin, "and still I stand ready with all my heart, to excuse and forgive them for adhering so strictly to an ancient celebration."

Catlin grew up near the Susquehanna River in Pennsylvania. Perhaps he dreamed of traveling down it. As an adult, he would spend many months aboard riverboats, which carried him to the Native American tribes far to the west.

CHAPTER TWO

The Early Years

The plows in my father's fields were
daily turning up Indian skulls or Indian bones,
and Indian flint arrow-heads.
—*George Catlin*

The Catlin family had come to America during the mid-seventeenth century. They first settled in Litchfield, Connecticut, in 1664. George Catlin's father, Putnam, was born exactly one hundred years later in Litchfield. When Putnam was only a boy, the American colonies declared their independence from Great Britain. After his father joined the Revolutionary Army, Putnam also volunteered. He became a fifer, playing music to keep the army's soldiers marching in step. He served until the war was over.

Following the war, Putnam Catlin returned to Litchfield where he studied law. But the area had become so heavily settled that there were few opportunities for a young man. Like so many other young men at that time, Putnam decided to head west. His destination was Wilkes-Barre, a growing community located on the Susquehanna River in northeastern Pennsylvania. Since there were few roads in the West, settlers and traders relied on the rivers to carry them from one place to another. When Putnam arrived in Wilkes-Barre in 1787, it was a thriving center of trade with plenty of work for a young lawyer.

Soon after arriving in Wilkes-Barre, Putnam Catlin met Polly Sutton. The Suttons had lived in the area during the American Revolution, when Wilkes-Barre had been the scene of a terrible Indian massacre. Polly's father had escaped the massacre by swimming across the Susquehanna River. But Polly and her mother had been captured by Oneida Indians. They remained captives for a short time until being rescued by an American army that invaded the Oneida lands.

After their marriage in 1789, Polly and Putnam Catlin had fourteen children—twelve boys and two girls. George, the fifth oldest, was born on July 26, 1796. While George was still a child, his father moved the family from Wilkes-Barre to a farm about forty miles away along the banks of the Susquehanna River. George later wrote that the farm was in a "picturesque little valley" that had been the scene of many Indian battles. "The plows in my father's fields were daily turning up Indian skulls or Indian bones, and Indian flint arrow-heads."

When George was about ten years old, he saw his first Indian. George had taken an old shotgun into the woods to hunt deer. As he was walking along, a large male deer appeared ahead of him. George quietly took aim and prepared to pull the trigger. But before he could get off a shot, someone else fired, killing the buck. George saw an Indian walk into the clearing to claim his prey. At first, George was frightened that the Indian might attack him, and he even thought about killing the man. "I saw then—though a child—in the momentary glance of that face, what infant human nature could not fail to see, and none but human nature could express," he wrote. "I saw humanity."

George went home and reported the incident to his father, who decided to go out and investigate. Putnam and his son eventually found the Indian's campsite in the woods. They discovered that he was an Oneida warrior named On-o-gong-way— which means the Great Warrior—who was traveling with his wife and ten-year-old daughter. The Great Warrior said that his father had participated in the massacre at Wilkes-Barre many years earlier.

When the Indians were driven north by white soldiers, the Great Warrior's father had stopped to bury a large golden kettle. On-o-gong-way had returned to find it. At this point, Putnam sent his son back to their farmhouse to bring back a kettle that had been discovered in one of the fields. When the boy returned, On-o-gong-way recognized the kettle—although it was made of copper, not gold, as he had remembered.

The Great Warrior and his family remained for a few days on the Catlin's land. He made a bow, some arrows, and a quiver for George. Then On-o-gong-way and his family headed on their way. A short time later, his body was found, shot twice, probably by settlers.

Off to School

In 1808, the Catlins moved to Hopbottom, Pennsylvania. There, George, along with two of his brothers, attended elementary school. They learned mathematics, English

Polly Catlin, George's mother, was captured by Oneida Indians when she was a girl and later released. Although we do not have details about her captivity, we know she was not harmed and that her son did not feel resentment toward the Oneidas.

Mrs. Putnam Catlin (Mary "Polly" Sutton). George Catlin, 1835

George Catlin spent his boyhood on a farm such as this one, near Wilkes-Barre. The bustling town had been founded in 1769, when Pennsylvania was a colony, in the region that was first inhabited by the Shawnee and the Delaware.

The Grave of William Penn. Edward Hicks, c. 1847

grammar, Latin, and Greek. These courses were part of the standard American education in the early nineteenth century. But George later admitted that he was not a particularly good student and spent most of his time "with books reluctantly held in one hand, and a rifle or fishing pole firmly and affectionately grasped in the other."

His father, however, had other plans for him. Putnam wanted George to follow in his footsteps and become a lawyer. In 1817, George was sent to the Reeve and Gould school of law in Litchfield, Connecticut. It was considered one of the finest law schools in the United States. Classes were conducted by Judges Tapping Reeve and James Gould.

When George arrived in Litchfield, it was almost like being home again. Some of his cousins lived in the community. One cousin, Grove Catlin, ran a local tavern. His daughter, Flora, was a drawing teacher at a Litchfield women's academy.

While he was supposed to be studying law, George had begun to spend some of his time drawing. Flora recognized his talent and encouraged him to practice. During the year he spent in Litchfield, George sharpened his skills and even painted a portrait of Judge Reeve.

Law and Painting

In 1818, George was back in Wilkes-Barre after finishing a year at law school. Before he left, his father had said, "I wish I could promise you a second year in Litchfield; it will not be well in my power; you must therefore get as much legal science as possible while there." In a single year, George had received a great deal of training and was ready to open his own legal practice.

But only part of his mind was focused on law. The rest of the time, he was doing something else. "During this time," he recalled, "another and stronger passion was getting the advantage of me, that of painting, to which all my [love of the law] soon gave way; and after having covered nearly every inch of the lawyer's table . . . with penknife, pen and ink, and pencil sketches of judges, jurors, and culprits and spectators, I very deliberately resolved to convert my law library into paint pots and brushes and to pursue painting as my future, and apparently more agreeable profession."

By 1820, Catlin had moved to Philadelphia where he opened an artist's studio. At this time, there were no formal art schools in America where Catlin could receive training. He could only look at the works of other artists, try to learn from them, and constantly improve his techniques. Fortunately, Catlin was born with a gift for painting, which his cousin had recognized in Litchfield.

Catlin's specialty was painting miniature portraits. People often carried small por-

While George Catlin was away at law school, his father wrote to him regularly. Putnam Catlin was a busy man. He had a farm and a law practice, and he also had been elected to the state legislature. But he always had time for his son George.

"You are now placed more favorably for study and the improvement of your mind than you could be at any other place in the United States," he told George in one letter. "You must accustom yourself to public speaking and study that kind of oratory and logic which is suited to being a lawyer." He added in another letter, "you will have excellent examples before you, and will I hope deserve and experience the aid of gentlemen near you who will kindly afford you a helping hand. It is an arduous struggle you have to encounter, but the prize before you is of immense value."

Judge Tapping Reeve (Lawschool Founder/Teacher), Artist unknown, 1818

Judge Tapping Reeve is shown in this etching done in 1818, when Catlin was a student at his law school.

traits as reminders of their loved ones in the days before photographs were invented. George soon became quite well known in Philadelphia as an expert in painting miniatures and full-length portraits. Although his father may have been disappointed that George had given up law, he seemed to understand his son's decision. "My dear George," he wrote in 1821, "I am pleased that you have at length resolved to attempt portraits. . . . Most painters of eminence have worked at portraits and history."

Among these artists was Charles Wilson Peale, considered one of the most renowned portrait painters of the nineteenth century. Peale had painted George Washington, Thomas Jefferson, and other American leaders. Peale and his sons—who also were artists—were friends of Catlin and admirers of his paintings.

Peale owned a museum in Philadelphia where he had hung 200 of his portraits, charging 25¢ for visitors to come into the museum to view his works. One of these visitors was George Catlin. He saw not only Charles Wilson Peale's portraits but also sketches made by his son Titian Peale. In 1819, the young artist had accompanied an expedition west into the Rocky Mountains. Along the way, Titian made drawings of Indian tribes living there. These may have influenced Catlin to consider his own trip west to paint the Indians.

Early in 1823, a group of Indians on their way to Washington, D.C., stopped at Peale's Museum in Philadelphia. Catlin saw them and was struck by "their classic beauty . . . exactly for the painter's palette." While Catlin's career had been successful, he was gradually becoming bored painting portraits of the wealthy citizens of Philadelphia. Suddenly, a new opportunity seemed to open up in front of him.

"Man in the simplicity and loftiness of his nature . . . is surely the most beautiful model for the painter. . . . nothing short of the loss of my life shall prevent me from visiting their country, and of becoming their historian," Catlin said. It was a task "worthy of the life-time of one man." His life's work was about to begin.

Before Catlin's portraits, American artists did not portray Indians, such as this Oneida, very realistically.

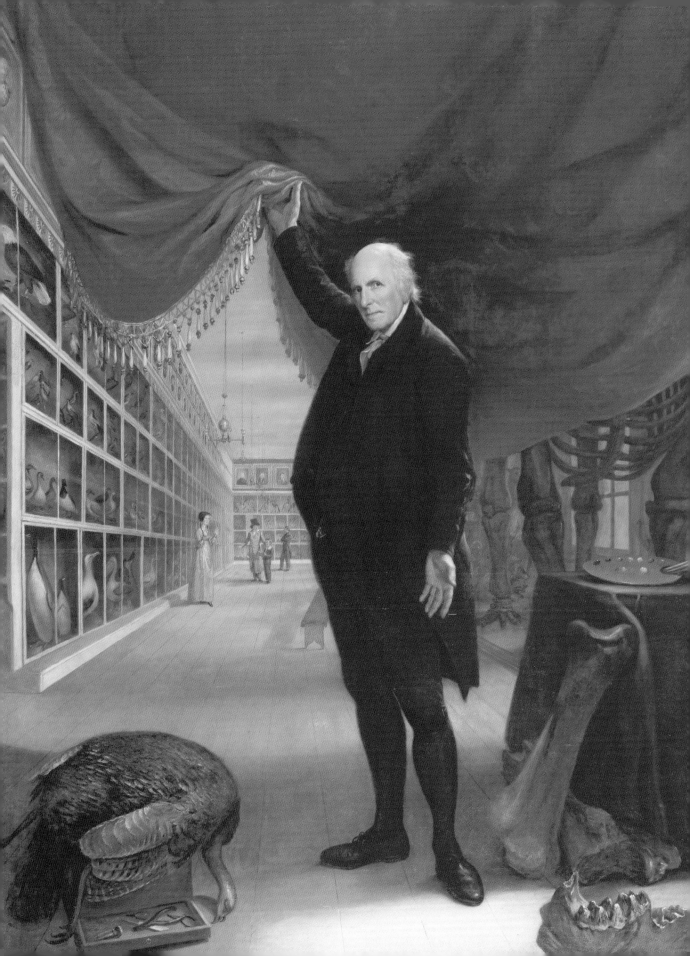

Opposite: Charles Wilson Peale founded the museum in Philadelphia where Catlin saw a group of Indians visiting from the West.

Buffalo Hunt on the River Platte. Titian Ramsey Peale, 1873

This painting of a buffalo hunt is by Titian Peale, Charles Wilson Peale's son. Titian Peale's depictions of Indians from the Rocky Mountains influenced the young George Catlin and inspired him to set out on his own westward journey.

Catlin fascinated the Indians with his realistic portraits of them on canvas.

CHAPTER THREE

Beginning a Life's Work

The operations of my brush are mysteries of the highest order
to these red sons of the prairie, and my room the earliest and
latest place of concentration of these wild and jealous spirits,
who all meet here to be amused and pay me signal honours.
—*George Catlin*

George Catlin knew what he wanted to do, but actually doing it was another matter. Traveling west to paint Native Americans cost money. And Catlin had very little to spare. As a result, he planned to continue painting portraits until he could save enough to put his plans into action.

In December 1824, Catlin traveled from Philadelphia to Albany, the capital of New York. There he was introduced to Governor De Witt Clinton and painted a miniature portrait of him. Clinton was among the most powerful politicians in the United States. In 1812, he had run for president, losing the election to James Madison. During his first term as governor, Clinton had directed the building of the Erie Canal, the great waterway connected the Great Lakes to the Hudson River and New York City.

Governor Clinton was impressed with Catlin's skill as a painter and introduced him to other well-to-do New York residents who wanted their portraits painted. The young artist was also a regular guest at the governor's mansion. During one of the gala parties there, Catlin met Clara Bartlett Gregory, an attractive, dark-haired woman from Albany. Clara was attracted to the handsome Catlin and fascinated by his plan to paint Native Americans. The couple was married in Albany on May 10, 1828. Although George's father was unable to make the long trip to Albany, he was delighted that his son was married.

"My dear George and my dear Clara," he wrote, "Most sincerely do I wish you much joy." Then he added for George, "I will anticipate seeing you very happy as a husband, with a wife looking over your shoulder, encouraging and admiring the arts. . . . Take good care of Clara and love her as much as you please."

Meanwhile, Catlin had already begun his work painting American Indians. He had visited an Indian reservation in upper New York State. The Iroquois had agreed to sell their lands and move onto this reservation. During his visit, Catlin painted the Seneca leader, Red Jacket.

Catlin's enthusiasm for painting Indians was shared by his younger brother Julius, who also was an artist. Several years earlier Julius had attended the United States Military Academy at West Point, New York. After graduation in 1824, Julius had been sent to Fort Gibson, on the western frontier in Arkansas. This gave him an opportunity to study the culture of Native Americans.

But Julius was unhappy serving in the army and resigned in 1826. He then headed east to join his brother George. About this time, Catlin was completing another portrait of Governor Clinton in Albany. This one had been commissioned by the Franklin Institute of Rochester, New York. After its completion, George asked Julius if he would deliver it to Rochester. Along the way, Julius went swimming in the Genesee River near the city. Tragically, the young man drowned—an incident that had a lasting impact on George because he blamed himself for his brother's death.

Nevertheless, Catlin continued painting Indians on the reservations in New York. Meanwhile, he was preparing for his first trip westward, which the artist hoped to begin in 1829. Unfortunately, Catlin's health was poor, and Clara fell sick as well. This forced him to postpone his plans. Instead the couple traveled south to Virginia, where the climate was warmer. Throughout his life, Catlin suffered from weak lungs that would undermine his physical stamina. But he refused to let poor health prevent him from working. In Virginia, Catlin painted a miniature portrait of Dolley Madison, wife of the former president.

Once Catlin and his wife had recovered their health, the artist traveled to Washington, D.C. Known as a respected portrait painter, he was able to meet with government officials. From them, he received letters of introduction to important men in St. Louis. This bustling trading center on the Mississippi River was the gateway to the West. Catlin hoped that with these letters he could persuade people in St. Louis to introduce him to an Indian leader, whom he wanted to paint.

Heading West

In 1830, Catlin and his wife went to Albany. Although she had not completely recovered, George intended to leave Clara with her father. It was a decision that many of his friends

Erie Canal. George Catlin, 1826

Catlin made this sketch of the construction of the Erie Canal.

Governor De Witt Clinton of New York directed the building of the Erie Canal. Catlin's miniature portrait of the influential Governor Clinton helped increase the young artist's reputation.

De Witt Clinton, Governor of New York. George Catlin, c. 1825

GENERAL WILLIAM CLARK
(1770–1838)

No white man knew more about Native Americans than William Clark. In 1803, he had joined Meriwether Lewis to lead an expedition to explore the lands acquired by the United States under the Louisiana Purchase. This vast territory, which doubled the size of the United States, was purchased for pennies an acre by President Thomas Jefferson from the French government.

Lewis and Clark led the members of the expedition, known as the Corps of Discovery, westward from St. Louis along the Missouri River and across the Rocky Mountains to the Pacific coast. Along the way, Clark made maps of the territory and made notes about the plants and animals.

After his return from the over 8,000-mile exploration, Clark became Superintendent of Indian Affairs, with his headquarters in St. Louis. He remained there for almost twenty-five years. As one writer put it, "No man could travel [west] without his permission. He was responsible for the whole Western Territory and its Indian population."

General William Clark. George Catlin, 1832

Catlin painted General William Clark, the Superintendent of Indian Affairs, who became the artist's mentor and arranged for him to paint some of his first portraits of Indians.

and family did not support. They believed that George was making a grave mistake in giving up his successful career painting portraits and leaving his wife to head west.

"I opened my views to my friends and relations," he later wrote, "but got not one advocate. . . . I broke from them all . . . myself my only adviser and protector."

In summer 1830, Catlin traveled to Cincinnati, located on the Ohio River. There he boarded a steamboat and went southward to the junction of the Ohio and the Mississippi rivers. From this point in Illinois, the steamboat headed north to St. Louis.

In 1830, St. Louis was a growing city of more than 7,000 people. Many of them were merchants and fur traders, who purchased beaver fur from the Indians in return for a wide variety of goods. These included colorful blankets, which had been made in England and shipped to New Orleans at the southern end of the Mississippi River, then taken north on flat boats to St. Louis. There also were iron pots, axes, and knives as well as beautiful glass beads. The beads had been made in Italy and shipped across the Atlantic Ocean.

All of these goods were stored in warehouses on the Mississippi River for shipment westward as part of the Indian trade. Large companies, such as the Rocky Mountain Fur Company and the American Fur Company, controlled the beaver trade in the West. They had established forts along the Missouri River and farther westward, which were centers of the fur trade. Beaver fur was in huge demand throughout the United States and Europe, where it was made into fashionable fur hats and warm winter coats.

When Catlin arrived in St. Louis, he planned to meet as soon as possible with General William Clark, the Superintendent of Indian Affairs. Catlin prepared very carefully for his first meeting with the sixty-year-old Clark. The artist brought along several of his Indian portraits, as well as other works. Clark was apparently impressed with Catlin's talent. He also recognized the artist's enthusiasm for painting American Indians. But perhaps most significantly, Clark admired the fact that Catlin was asking for no financial help from the government—he planned to finance all his travels himself.

Soon after Catlin arrived in St. Louis, General Clark posed for a full-length portrait by the young artist. Clark also recommended to his well-to-do friends in St. Louis that they consider having their portraits painted by Catlin. This would enable Catlin to earn money and finance his travels along the frontier. Meanwhile, Indian chiefs were visiting General Clark daily. They came to talk about the treaties signed by the tribes with the U.S. government and violations of these treaties by white traders.

Clark arranged for Catlin to sit in on these conversations, accompanied by his brushes and paints. Catlin had the ability to sketch a portrait very quickly. "In addition," according to historian Harold McKracken, "he had an unusual photographic memory which he relied on for finishing the picture later. Besides that, the Indians instinctively liked Catlin . . . and General Clark was undoubtedly well aware of this. The young artist not only became launched on his mission, but also gained the general's complete approval and friendship."

During July 1830, General Clark took Catlin along on a trip to Fort Crawford, north of St. Louis on the Mississippi River. As Clark met with local tribal chiefs, Catlin continued sketching. Among the Indians whom Catlin painted was Kee-o-kuk, known as the Running Fox, chief of the Sauks and Foxes. During the fall, Catlin continued his travels. He went to Fort Leavenworth in what would later become northeastern Kansas. At a meeting of the Iowa, Delaware, Shawnee, and other tribes, he made sketches of their chiefs. Among these chiefs were No Heart, chief of the Iowa, and He Who Goes Up the River, chief of the Shawnee.

Clara Bartlett Gregory Catlin (Mrs. George). George Catlin, c. 1828

Clara Catlin always seemed to understand her husband's single-minded devotion to his work. He left Clara behind in Albany during his travels to the West.

George Catlin arrived in St. Louis in 1830. St. Louis was called the "Gateway to the West," because many people started up the Missouri River from St. Louis on their way west. It was also called "Mound City," after the Indian burial mounds upon which the city was built.

INDIAN REMOVAL

During the first part of the nineteenth century, many Indian tribes sold their lands east of the Mississippi River and moved westward. These included bands of Shawnees and Sauks and Foxes, who had lived in the Ohio region. In 1830, Congress passed the Indian Removal Act.

The new law provided money to President Andrew Jackson so that he could pay several Indian tribes for their lands and encourage them to move across the Mississippi River to the Oklahoma Territory.

These tribes included the Cherokee, Choctaw, Creek, Seminole, and Chickasaw. Although some of the tribes moved voluntarily, others were forced westward by the United States Army.

During the 1830s, approximately 4,000 Indians died during this forced removal. As a result, the route they followed to Oklahoma was known as the Trail of Tears.

In a visit to the Konza [Kansas] tribe in fall 1830, Catlin painted a group of warriors, along with a woman and her child. The warriors wore fancy headdresses and rows of beads around their necks. One of them carried a large shield and a bow and arrow. After his journeys, Catlin returned to his artist's studio in St. Louis to finish his paintings. Then, late in the fall, he went back east to rejoin his wife, Clara, in Albany.

However, Catlin stayed only a short time before returning to the West. While Clara seemed to understand her husband's desire to continue his work—even if it meant leaving her—Putnam Catlin felt differently. "We can hardly conceive how you can well bear the separation for the winter," he wrote, "or that you can both be contented." George Catlin's dedication to his mission often meant that he put his own needs ahead of those of Clara or the opinions of his father. Some called it selfishness; others said it was stubbornness. But there was no doubt that Catlin put his work first.

In 1831, he was off on another journey. This one probably took him up the Platte River. There he painted portraits of Oto, Omaha, and Grand Pawnee Indians. Among these pictures are La-doo-ke-a of the Grand Pawnee. Catlin also painted Om-pah-ton-ga, chief of the Omaha, holding a long war club and wearing a large silver medallion around his neck.

By the time he returned east late in 1831, Catlin had finished the first stages of his plan to paint the Indians of the West. But this was only the beginning. Over the following four years, he would record events that no other artist had ever seen.

Konza Tribe. George Catlin, 1850

Catlin would quickly sketch his subjects, such as this group of Konza warriors, a woman, and her child. He would carefully roll up his drawings and take them back to his studio, where he had time to turn them into finished paintings. Catlin had an astounding ability to recall detail and color.

Opposite: Om-pah-tah-ga, an Omaha warrior, posed for his portrait in 1832. In the late 1700s and early 1800s, the Omaha dominated the Great Plains. They never fought with whites but battled the Sioux, who were driven by settlers into Omaha territory from the north. Nebraska's biggest city, Omaha, is named after them.

Catlin painted a picture of himself and his Indian guide, disguised by white wolf skins, as they approached a buffalo herd. "The mode in which these Indians kill this noble animal is spirited and thrilling in the extreme. . . . I have almost daily accompanied parties of Indians to see the fun, and have often shared in it myself."

CHAPTER FOUR

Painting the West

> I have roamed about from time to time during seven or
> eight years, visiting and associating with, some three or four
> hundred thousand of these people and . . . I feel bound to
> pronounce them, by nature, a kind and hospitable people.
> —*George Catlin*

"In the spring of 1832," Catlin wrote, "I ascended the Missouri on the steamer, *Yellow Stone.*" A large steamboat with a side-wheel and two large black smokestacks, the *Yellow Stone* had been built by the American Fur Company. It was designed to carry a large supply of trading goods to the company's posts in the West. Starting out from St. Louis, Catlin traveled on the *Yellow Stone* west and then north up the Missouri River to its junction with the Yellowstone River. This was the site of Fort Union, the American Fur Company's westernmost trading post in what is today western North Dakota.

Almost all the people traveling on the *Yellow Stone* were the American Fur Company's traders and trappers. But during his trip to St. Louis, Catlin had met Pierre Chouteau, manager of the company. The artist realized that a trip on the *Yellow Stone* offered an unusual opportunity for him to paint the Indians of the West. Catlin persuaded Chouteau, who was impressed with the artist's work, to let him come aboard for the steamboat's first voyage.

Among the passengers was Major John Sanford, the U.S. Indian Agent for the Upper Missouri River. He was returning from Washington, D.C., with a group of Indians who had been visiting President Andrew Jackson. Among them was Pigeon's Egg Head, a member of the Assiniboine tribe. Catlin had painted him in St. Louis months earlier as he was leaving for the East. As Catlin wrote, the Indian was dressed

INDIAN NAMES

Native Americans were given names by their families. They also often were given a second name, which described a characteristic or event for which they were known. Whites wrote these sounds as they heard them, so spellings vary. They then translated the names into English. For example, Mah-to-toh-pah, a chief of the Mandan, was called Four Bears, and Wi-jun-jon became Pigeon's Egg Head. Actually, Catlin made a mistake when he recorded Wi-jun-jon's name. He was really called Ah-jon-jon, meaning the Light. But Pigeon's Egg Head is the name that stuck.

Fort Pierre, Mouth of the Teton River, 1200 Miles above St. Louis. George Catlin, 1832

"On my way up the river," wrote Catlin, "I made a painting of this lovely spot, taken from the summit of the bluffs, a mile or two distant, showing an encampment of Sioux, of six hundred tents or skin lodges, around the Fort, where they had concentrated to make their spring trade; exchanging their furs and [pelts] for articles and luxuries of civilized manufactures."

in "his native costume, which was classic and exceedingly beautiful; his leggings and shirt were of mountain goat skin, richly garnished with quills of the porcupine and fringed with the locks of scalps taken from his enemies' heads . . . his head was decked with the war eagles' plumes, his robe was of the skin of a young buffalo bull, decorated with scenes of the battles of his life."

When Pigeon's Egg Head returned from Washington, he had exchanged his native costume for a U.S. Army uniform. Instead of a headdress, he wore a tall beaver hat with a red feather, and he carried a blue umbrella. Catlin painted the Indian in his new clothing and put it alongside with the previous portrait—a sort of "before and after."

Among the Sioux

During spring 1832, the *Yellow Stone* chugged along the muddy, churning Missouri River. On the plains, Catlin could see vast herds of buffalo, as well as other animals such as deer and elk. The river itself was filled with tree limbs and other debris, which had to be pushed aside for the steamboat to continue its voyage. As the ship passed Indian villages, the crew fired the boat's cannon. This scared the Indians, who called

CATLIN AND THE TRADERS

The U.S. Congress had passed a law prohibiting traders from taking alcohol to the Indian tribes. Nevertheless, General Clark had permitted the *Yellow Stone* to carry a supply of whiskey westward. Clark was involved in the fur trade and realized that liquor was a very effective trading item. As the steamboat stopped along the Missouri River at the village of the Ponca tribe, Catlin talked to one of the chiefs about the effects of alcohol on his people. The chief said that, under the influence of "fire-water," the Indians had allowed white hunters to kill off most of the buffalo in the region.

Buffalo hides were made into robes that were very popular among people in the eastern cities. Catlin also listened to the traders aboard the *Yellow Stone* brag about how many beaver skins they could purchase for a single bottle of whiskey.

Catlin denounced the whiskey trade and its effect on the Indians: "So long as the past and present system of trade and whiskey-selling is tolerated amongst them, there is little hope for their improvement, nor any chance for more than a temporary existence."

"There were many curious conjectures amongst their wise men, with regard to the nature and powers of the steam-boat," wrote Catlin. "Amongst the Mandans, some called it the 'big thunder canoe'; for when in distance below the village, they saw the lightning flash from its sides, and heard the thunder come from it; others called it the 'big medicine canoe with eyes'; it was medicine [mystery] because they could not understand it; and it must have eyes, for said they, 'it sees its own way, and takes the deep water in the middle of the channel.' "

Opposite: Pigeon's Egg Head left for Washington dressed in "his native costume," according to Catlin, but returned from his negotiations dressed as a white man.

the *Yellow Stone* the Big Medicine Canoe with Eyes. From the deck, Catlin sketched the Indian villages as well as the magnificent landscape along the river.

Finally, the Missouri River became so shallow that the *Yellow Stone* was grounded on a sandbar. Chouteau decided to lead a group of men 200 miles across the plains to the American Fur Company's post at Fort Pierre. Located farther up the Missouri River, it was named after Pierre Chouteau. Catlin accompanied the expedition with his sketchbook and paints. After reaching the fort, he set up a small studio and began to work. One of his paintings was a panorama of Fort Pierre, surrounded by hundreds of tepees belonging to the Sioux.

Catlin began painting the Sioux chiefs. His first portrait was a picture of One Horn, first chief of the Sioux. At first, when the other Indians saw the portrait, they were afraid to let Catlin paint their pictures. The Sioux were frightened by the stunning portrait of One Horn, looking straight out from the canvas. They feared that the chief's spirit had been captured by the painting. The tribe's medicine men claimed that the chief would never close his eyes or sleep again. They called Catlin the Medicine Painter because they believed he possessed strong medicine—great power. But One Horn reassured his people that no harm would come to him or anyone else from having their portraits painted.

His reassuring words convinced other chiefs to sit for their portraits. Catlin worked quickly, sketching and adding a few paints to create the broad outlines of the portraits. His colors included vermillion [red], blue-green, and blue. He also made notes in his sketchbook to help him finish the portraits later. Then he rolled up each canvas and put the partly completed painting into a metal tube to protect it.

The chiefs were so impressed with his work that they held a special Dance of the Chieftains to honor him. Catlin sketched not only this dance but others as well. One of these was the Bear Dance, put on by hunters before they went out to kill bear. Bear meat was a favorite food among the Sioux, who also smeared bear grease on their long hair and their bodies. Catlin also sketched a Scalp Dance, which honored warriors who brought home enemy scalps after a battle.

One of the portraits painted by Catlin was a profile of Little Bear, a Sioux chief. When another Sioux, known as Dog, saw the portrait, he laughed and said that it showed Little Bear was only half a man. This angered Little Bear and eventually led to a shoot-out between the two men. Dog shot Little Bear, who died soon afterward. This created an uproar among the Sioux, many of whom blamed Catlin for the incident. Fortunately, by that time the *Yellow Stone* had steamed upriver to Fort Pierre. Catlin and the other travelers quickly left the fort and continued their journey.

Fort Union

The next stop was Fort Union, on the Missouri River, many miles from St. Louis. Along the way the *Yellow Stone* stopped at an Assiniboine village, which was the home of Pigeon's Egg Head. "I saw him walk ashore," Catlin wrote, "with a keg of whiskey under his arm and blue umbrella in his hand." At first, his family and friends pretended not to recognize him because of his clothes. Eventually, they began to welcome him and listen to his stories of the trip to Washington, D.C. Unfortunately, Pigeon's Egg Head never stopped telling the stories. Instead of resuming his former role in the village, he did little more than drink alcohol and talk. Gradually, the tribe grew tired of him because he never stopped telling his stories, and the other Indians thought that many of them were lies. Eventually, they killed him.

Fort Union was located where the Yellowstone joins the Missouri River. Soon after his arrival there, Catlin painted a picture of the fort and a large encampment of Indians outside its walls. These included Blackfeet, Crows, Assiniboines, and Crees. While these tribes were often bitter enemies, they agreed to get along with each other when trading at Fort Union. Catlin set up a studio in one part of the fort, using the end of a cannon as his artist's chair. So many Indians wanted to be painted that Catlin had to ask the chiefs to select those "worthy of so high an honor."

CATLIN AT FORT UNION

"I have this day been painting a portrait of the head chief of the Blackfoot nation . . . Stu-mick-o-such. Whilst sitting for his picture he has been surrounded by his own braves and warriors, and also gazed at by his enemies . . . a number of distinguished personages of each of which tribes have laid all day around the sides of my room; reciting to each other the battles they have fought, and pointing to the scalp locks worn as proofs of their victories, and attached to the seams of their shirts and leggings. . . .

I have also painted Pe-toh-pee-kis, the Eagle Ribs. . . . Of all the Blackfeet whose portraits are now standing in my room, he is one of the most extraordinary. Though not a chief, he stands here in the Fort and deliberately boasts of eight scalps which he says he has taken from the heads of trappers and traders with his own hands. Each year the Blackfeet killed some of these white men, whom they accused of killing off too many animals and jeopardizing the tribe's food supply."

"[The Sioux] live in a country well-stocked with buffaloes and wild horses, which furnish them an excellent and easy living," wrote Catlin. "Their atmosphere is pure, which produces good health and long life; and they are the most independent and the happiest races of Indians I have met with."

Opposite: In 1832, Catlin painted a medicine man of the Blackfeet Indians trying to save the life of a dying chief.

While Catlin was staying at Fort Union, one of the Cree warriors shot and killed a chief of the Blackfeet. As the chief lay dying, the tribal medicine man, dressed in a yellow bear skin, danced over him and prayed to the Great Spirit. Catlin captured this ritual on canvas, showing the medicine man shaking a large rattle over the chief's body and carrying a long medicine spear.

While staying at Fort Union, Catlin traveled onto the plains, where he painted the buffalo. On one expedition, he was accompanied by one of the Indians. Both men were covered in wolf skins to camouflage themselves. From underneath his skin, Catlin sketched the animals. He also painted Indians on horseback hunting buffalo. As they rode among the huge herds, the Indians separated one of the buffalo from the rest of the animals. Riding along the right side of the buffalo, a hunter shot an arrow into its heart, bringing the huge animal down.

The herds of buffalo were enormous, but Catlin could foresee the day when the white men and the Indians might hunt them to extinction. He was afraid that if that happened, the Indians' way of life might vanish. "What a splendid contemplation it would be," he wrote, "by some great protecting policy of our government, to preserve them in their pristine beauty and wildness, in a *magnificent park*, where the world could see them for ages to come. . . . A *National Park*, containing man and beast, in all the wild freshness of their native beauty! I would ask no other monument to my memory, than to be the founder of such an institution."

Return Trip to St. Louis

By the end of July 1832, Catlin was beginning his return journey by canoe from Fort Union to St. Louis. He was accompanied by two employees of the American Fur Company who were experienced in river travel. Catlin also was joined by a magnificent eagle, which had been given to him as a gift by Kenneth McKenzie, who was in charge of Fort Union. The bird sat on a high perch that had been erected over the canoe.

Near Fort Clark, located on the Missouri River, Catlin stopped at the villages of the Mandan tribe. The Mandan built large circular dome-shaped lodges of wood, covered with willow boughs and clay. One day, Catlin climbed to the top of a Mandan lodge from where he sketched the entire village. His picture showed some of the villagers sitting on their roofs talking with each other or just enjoying the bright summer sunshine.

Catlin painted many portraits of the Mandans, some of whom had blue eyes and blond hair. Among his pictures was a portrait of Four Bears, a Mandan chief, who admired Catlin's work and invited him to a large banquet of buffalo meat. He also painted Mink, a beautiful Mandan woman.

Catlin painted this panorama of the villages of the Mandan located along the Missouri River. "These people formerly (and within the recollection of many of their oldest men) lived fifteen or twenty miles farther down the river, in ten contiguous villages; the marks or ruins of which are yet plainly to be seen. At that period, it is evident, as well from the number of lodges which their villages contained, as from their traditions, that their numbers were much greater than at the present day."

While he lived among the Mandan, Catlin recorded their way of life. As one of their favorite activities, the Indian men enjoyed taking steam baths. A Mandan woman placed a large basket on a wooden platform inside a tepee. Under the basket was a mat scented with herbs. Then she brought hot rocks from a nearby fire and placed them under the basket. These were drenched with water, which produced steam for the warrior sitting inside the basket. After enjoying the sweet-smelling steam, he quickly cooled off by jumping into a nearby river. Finally, he was rubbed down with bear grease.

Among their games, the Mandan loved horse racing. They also played the Game of Arrows, with each contestant trying to shoot as many arrows as possible into the air before one of them fell to the ground. Some Mardans could fire as many as eight arrows in that short period of time.

After leaving the Mandan, Catlin and his companions continued down the Missouri River. One day, they paddled among a large herd of buffalo swimming in the river. It was very dangerous because one of the huge animals could easily tip over the canoe, destroying all of Catlin's work and even killing the travelers.

"It was in the 'running season,' and we had heard the 'roaring' (as it was called) of the herd when we were several miles from it," Catlin wrote. "When we came in sight . . . the river was filled and in parts blackened with their heads and horns, as they were swimming about. . . . I deemed it imprudent for our canoe to be dodging amongst them and ran it ashore for a few hours, when we laid waiting for the river to clear, but we waited in vain. Their number, however, got somewhat diminished at last, and we pushed off, and successfully made our way amongst them."

By the time Catlin finally reached St. Louis, he had been traveling for eighty-six days and painted over 135 pictures. It was an incredible achievement.

After his return, Catlin continued painting. He went south of St. Louis to paint a portrait of Black Hawk, chief of the Sauk and Fox. Black Hawk had refused to accept a treaty with the U.S. government, in which he and his people would have to give up their territory and move westward. Instead he declared war. After Black Hawk was defeated, he was taken in chains, along with many other warriors, to a prison at Jefferson Barracks, ten miles from St. Louis. Catlin painted Black Hawk as well as another chief, known as the Prophet.

The First Exhibit

In December, after turning his rough sketches into finished paintings, Catlin headed east with his year's works. He met his wife, Clara, in Pittsburgh, Pennsylvania, located

Drinks the Juice of the Stone, in Ball-Player's Dress. Choctaw. George Catlin, 1834

Among the favorite games of the Indian tribes was lacrosse,
often played by large teams made up of hundreds of warriors.

on the Ohio River. Catlin spent a restless winter because he had become very sick with a lung illness.

After his recovery, George and Clara prepared an exhibition of his paintings. The exhibit, which began in April 1833, was criticized by the *Pittsburgh Gazette*. The newspaper said of his paintings that "Most of them are in an unfinished state, he only having had sufficient leisure to secure correct likenesses." Some of the people who came to the exhibit called the paintings "crude."

But Catlin and his wife were not discouraged by this reaction. Instead, they took the exhibit to Cincinnati, Ohio. There, the editor of the *Western Monthly Magazine* called the exhibit "the most extraordinary and interesting that we have ever witnessed, and one which constitutes a most valuable addition to the history of our continent, as well as to the arts of our country." After the exhibit closed in the fall, the Catlins traveled to Pensacola, Florida, where George's brother James lived. George Catlin found the warm winters there were better for his health.

More Journeys

Poor health did not prevent George Catlin from setting out on another painting expedition among the Indians. After leaving Clara in New Orleans, he headed up the Mississippi River toward Fort Gibson on the Arkansas River in 1834. Catlin had obtained permission to accompany a military expedition that was traveling westward to explore the Rocky Mountains. It was Catlin's first visit to Fort Gibson, where his brother Julius had been posted several years earlier.

After arriving at the fort, Catlin began painting some of the Cherokees living there. The Indian Removal Act had forced them to leave their lands east of the Mississippi River.

Located around Fort Gibson were villages of Osage and Choctaw Indians. The Choctaw enjoyed a game similar to lacrosse, which Catlin captured on canvas. On the day before the game, thousands of Indians gathered on the playing field. They erected goal posts at either end of the field, then began making bets on which team would win the game.

The next day several hundred ball players gathered, each of them carrying two sticks with a net at one end. As the judges threw a ball into the air and fired a gun, the game began. The Indians tried to catch the ball in one of their sticks and pass it down the field. The first team to make 100 goals was declared the winner.

In June 1834, Catlin headed west with the military expedition, which was led by Colonel Henry Dodge. Along the way, many of the men came down with a mysterious illness. Catlin himself became extremely sick, although he continued traveling. As they moved farther west, Catlin and the soldiers eventually encountered a large war-party of Comanches. Riding ahead of the other warriors was their leader, an Indian known as the Little Spaniard.

"This moment was the commencement of one of the most thrilling and beautiful scenes I ever witnessed," Catlin wrote. "On a beautiful and gently rolling prairie, he was reining and spurring and spurring his maddened horse, and gradually approaching us by tacking to the right and the left. . . . He at length came prancing and leaping along till he met the flag of the regiment, when he leaned his spear for a moment against it, looking the bearer full in the face, then he wheeled his horse and dashed up to Col. Dodge. His hand was extended which was instantly grasped and shaken."

The Little Spaniard and his men led the expedition to their village. Colonel Dodge eventually went westward toward the Rockies, but Catlin was too sick to make the journey. Instead he remained in the Comanche village, painting as much as possible,

Catlin painted the Little Spaniard, who raced ahead of a
Comanche war-party to greet Colonel Henry Dodge and
the military unit with whom Catlin traveled.

until Colonel Dodge returned. Then Catlin accompanied him back to Fort Gibson. By this time, the artist had begun to feel better, and he planned to leave the fort and return to St. Louis.

As Catlin's biographer Mark Sufrin wrote, "Everyone at the fort tried to discourage him, telling him he was far too weak, but he wouldn't change his mind. It was another test of his remarkable endurance." Catlin eventually reached St. Louis on his horse, Charley, and crossed the Mississippi River to Alton, Illinois, where Clara was staying. The couple then headed down the river to spend the winter in New Orleans.

The Last Trips

In spring 1835, George and Clara left New Orleans and returned to St. Louis. From there they traveled up the Mississippi River to Fort Snelling. Around this stone fort gathered the Sioux and Chippewa tribes. Catlin painted the Chippewa lodges made from long poles covered in birch bark. He also captured the Chippewa Snow-Shoe Dance, which commemorated the falling snow.

During the summer, Clara took a steamboat southward to Prairie du Chien and later to St. Louis. Catlin paddled a canoe down the river, stopping along the way to paint in Indian villages. Eventually, he reached Camp Des Moines, an important military post. Traveling outside the fort, Catlin visited the villages of the Sauk and Fox. After leaving Camp Des Moines, Catlin returned to St. Louis, and he and Clara headed east.

Clara, who was pregnant with the couple's first child, went to her parents' home in Albany. Meanwhile, Catlin was planning to present an exhibit of his paintings in Buffalo, New York. During the spring, however, Clara lost the child. Meanwhile, Catlin's father, Putnam, and two of his brothers had come up to Buffalo to help George prepare the exhibit. Suddenly, George announced that he was canceling the exhibition. A boat was leaving Buffalo for the West and George wanted to return to Indian country. His plan was to visit Pipestone Quarry, an area forbidden to white people.

As his great-niece, Marjorie Catlin Roehm, put it, "George's abrupt departure on this extremely dangerous trip into Indian country plainly showed one of his less happy traits of character: his complete unconcern for others if it interfered with his plans. His sick and grieving wife should have been enough to keep him home. . . . He left his valuable paintings in the hands of inexperienced persons. . . . He took it for granted that his aging father would see that everything was attended to."

Catlin left in July 1836, reaching Prairie du Chien by the end of the month. Pipestone Quarry, his destination, was a massive rock formation, located west of Fort

Snelling. From this quarry, which was sacred to the Indians, came the red clay for their peace pipes. Catlin traveled with a companion named Robert Wood. Along the way, they met a group of Sioux at a trading post, who warned them not to go to Pipestone. ". . . we know that no white man has ever been to the Pipestone Quarry, and our chiefs have often decided in council that no white man shall ever go to it," they told Catlin. "You have heard what I have to say and you can go no farther, but you must turn about and go back."

Catlin refused to listen and continued on his journey. For some reason, the Sioux allowed him to reach the quarry without harm. Once he arrived, Catlin began painting Pipestone Quarry, which contained a large wall of quartz on one side, stretching for two miles. The red pipestone lay beneath the soil inside the quarry. "I am encamped on . . . the very rock where the Great Spirit stood when he consecrated the *pipe of peace,* by molding it from the rock, and smoking it over the congregated nations that were assembled about him," he wrote.

After completing several days of painting at Pipestone Quarry, Catlin headed south to St. Louis by steamboat. Unfortunately, some of his paintings were stolen from the boat. Catlin could not help but draw a contrast between this experience and his travels among the Indians. During those journeys, nothing had been stolen. The Indians generally had treated him with great respect and courtesy, more so than his own people.

Catlin headed east to the home he shared with Clara in Albany. Although he did not realize it at the time, the artist had just completed his last trip among the Indian tribes of the West.

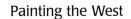

In 1837, Catlin completed his portraits and prepared to show them in an exhibition. This 1849 portrait of George Catlin is by William Fisk.

CHAPTER FIVE

The Wild West Show

An Indian world entirely different than anything seen
or painted before—a vast country where men are red;
where meat is the staff of life; where no laws but
those of honor are known.
—*George Catlin*

"Georg remains at Albany, detained by a severe illness for a week," Putnam Catlin wrote to his youngest son, Francis. Nevertheless, George continued to work. Putnam added, "Clara . . . says she wishes I could take a peep at him in his painting some day to see his dexterity with his brush and the effect of his re-touches, particularly of his landscapes and unfinished [Indian] groups, from morn till night."

Catlin was preparing to open the exhibition of his entire collection of paintings, as well as the Indian tools, weapons, and clothing that he had collected. Following his illness, Catlin showed the exhibition, called the Indian Gallery, in Albany, and then in Troy, New York. Then he took the exhibit to New York City, where it opened on September 25, 1837. Catlin's exhibition was the first Wild West Show ever staged in the United States. It not only included his portraits and items collected from the Indian villages, but some of the Native Americans themselves appeared at the exhibition.

The exhibitions in New York City were extremely successful. On November 1, 1837, approximately 1,500 people filled the exhibit hall to see a special appearance by Chief Kee-o-kuk and twenty members of the Sauk and Fox tribes. Catlin kept the exhibit open until the end of December. Although the crowds were still coming to Clinton Hall, Catlin decided to close the Wild West Show, at least for a while.

About this time, Clara gave birth to the couple's first daughter, Elizabeth. But this was not the reason that Catlin shut down his exhibit. He had decided to travel to

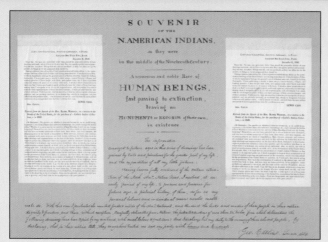
South Carolina, leaving his wife and new baby. Catlin had learned that Osceola, chief of the Seminole, had been imprisoned there in Fort Moultrie.

The Seminole chief had led a long struggle against the U.S. Army. In 1832, according to the Treaty of Paynes Landing, the Seminole people had agreed to leave their lands in Florida and live west of the Mississippi River. While some of the Seminoles moved, Osceola refused to go. The chief said that he would battle the white men "till the last drop of Seminole blood has moistened the dust of his hunting ground." A bloody war broke out and continued until 1837. Under a flag of peace, Osceola finally agreed to meet with the U.S Army. But army leaders violated the truce and captured the Seminole leader, along with about 250 members of his tribe, who were taken to Fort Moultrie.

When Catlin heard what had happened, he was outraged. The artist also wanted to paint a portrait of Osceola. After arriving at Fort Moultrie, Catlin learned that Osceola was very sick. Nevertheless, the chief agreed to sit for his portrait. "I have painted him precisely in the costume, in which he stood for his picture, even to a string and trinket. He wore three ostrich feathers in his head, and a turban made of a vari-colored cotton shawl. . . . he is a most extraordinary man and one entitled to a better fate." Shortly after Catlin finished the portrait, Osceola died.

Efforts to Sell the Exhibit

Catlin returned to New York and reopened his exhibit at Stuyvesant Hall, featuring the portrait of Osceola. Meanwhile, he was trying to convince the U.S. Congress to authorize the purchase of the Indian Gallery of paintings. Catlin believed that it would serve as an excellent tribute to the splendid culture of the Native American tribes. In April 1838, he even took the Indian Gallery to Washington, D.C., and opened a new exhibit. Many members of Congress were very impressed with Catlin's work. But others were strongly opposed to purchasing the collection.

Catlin had irritated many political leaders because of his comments about the white man's treatment of the Indians. In his lectures, he accused the white traders and trappers of using alcohol to swindle the Indians out of their furs and their lands. He said that the U.S. government had violated its peace treaties with the Indians and was destroying their culture. As a result, Congress refused to purchase the Gallery.

Catlin closed the exhibit in Washington, taking it to Baltimore, then Philadelphia, and finally to Boston in 1838. In Boston, the Gallery opened at Faneuil Hall, one of the city's most famous historic buildings. "His collection makes a fine show on the walls, and it elicits praise from all," his wife Clara wrote. "His portraits are becoming more valuable every day." But she added that if Congress did not decide to purchase the collection during 1839, "George will probably go to Europe early in the spring."

The following summer, after showing the exhibit in New York and Philadelphia, Catlin announced that he was taking it to Europe. He hoped that the press might put enough pressure on members of Congress to force them to purchase the collection. But nothing happened, and Catlin and his Gallery sailed for England in November 1839.

In England, Catlin prepared to open his exhibition at a large hall in London. He received assistance from an old friend named Charles Murray, whom the artist had met in the West. Murray was a highly placed official on the staff of England's Queen Victoria. He arranged for members of the nobility to see the exhibit before it opened to the public. Their enthusiastic comments about the paintings created great interest among the British people.

The response was enormous. The exhibit included 600 of Catlin's paintings, along with an Indian teepee and other cultural items. Hundreds of people came to see the

Chin-cha-pee, Fire Bug That Creeps, Wife of Pigeon's Egg Head. 1832

Little Wolf, a Famous Warrior. 1844

Great Chief, a Boy, Menomine;

"They are human beings, with features, thoughts, reason, and sympathies like our own."—George Catlin

Black Hawk, Prominent Sauk Chief. 1832

Osceola, the Black Drink, a Warrior of Great Distinction. Seminole. 1838

One Horn, Head Chief of the Miniconjou Tribe. 1832

Fast Dancer, a Warrior. Ojibway. 1834

PROTESTS FROM THE PRESS

When Catlin said he was taking his Indian Gallery to Europe, the newspapers reacted immediately.

The *United States Gazette* wrote "We have learned with great regret that he will certainly take his museum to England in the course of a few weeks. We know too well how it will be valued there, to imagine that it will ever be permitted to come back."

The *American Sentinel* added, "Mr. Catlin's extraordinary exhibition of Indian curiosities will be closed in a few days, as it will be taken to England at once and there disposed of. . . . No citizen should suffer it to leave this country."

And the *New York Evening Star* stated, "Nothing could rebound more to the patriotism, national pride, and honor of our country, than the purchase of this collection."

exhibit and listen to Catlin's lectures. Nothing like the Indian Gallery had ever before been seen in Europe.

Catlin was very pleased that the success he had not been able to achieve in the United States had finally come to him in England. As he wrote his parents, "I . . . have at last succeeded in making what they call 'a decided hit.'" But Catlin added that while he had made money on the exhibit, his expenses were also "very heavy" for renting the hall.

One of Catlin's happiest days in London was the arrival of Clara in June 1840. She brought their older daughter, Elizabeth, and their six-month-old daughter, Clara. Catlin had left the United States before she was born. As he put it, she "was like the coming of the warm and gentle breeze of spring." Catlin had found a home for his family just outside London. Then, in 1841, Catlin published a book in England. It was titled *Letters and Notes on the Manners, Customs, and Conditions of the North American Indians.* The book sold widely, and Catlin wrote to his father, "No book of the present age, it is said, has had so frequent and undivided applause."

Ups and Downs in England

Living in England and running the exhibit cost Catlin a large amount of money. Meanwhile, the size of the audiences grew smaller once many people had already seen the exhibition. Catlin eventually closed the gallery in London and took his exhibit to other English cities, including Liverpool and Manchester. In Liverpool, he met a group of Ojibway Indians who had been brought to England for a tour of the country. Catlin hurried back to London to reopen his exhibit with the Ojibways. This revived interest in the exhibition, which the artist had now turned into the Wild West Show he had begun in New York. The Wild West Show included not only Catlin's paintings and collected artifacts, but live Indians riding horses.

It was such a success that Catlin, his wife, and the Ojibways were invited to visit Queen Victoria. Bursting with pride, Catlin wrote about the visit to his parents. "To think that, from a little *go-to-mill boy* [a nobody] I have worked my way across the Atlantic, and at last into the Palace and presence of the Queen of England, and more than all that, received from her own lips her thanks for the interesting information which I had given her."

Even more exciting for Catlin was the birth of two more children—a daughter, named Victoria, and a son, George, Jr. Meanwhile, Catlin had published another book. Called the *North American Indian Portfolio: Hunting Scenes and Amusements of the Rocky Mountains and Prairies of America*, it was released in 1845.

By this time, Clara hoped that her husband might end his trip to England and bring their family home to New York. Catlin planned to leave and even announced that he was closing the exhibit. But his plans were changed by a group of Iowa Indians who had journeyed to London. Catlin had traveled among the Iowa in the West. When they asked for his help, he decided to put them into his Wild West Show. Some of the Indians became sick in London and died. Meanwhile, Catlin's expenses were rising, and attendance at the show continued to decline.

EXCERPT FROM *LETTERS AND NOTES . . . ON THE NORTH AMERICAN INDIANS*

"I have roamed about from time to time during seven or eight years, visiting and associating with, some three or four hundred thousand of these people . . . and from the very many and decided voluntary acts of their hospitality and kindness, I feel bound to pronounce them, by nature, a kind and hospitable people. I have been welcomed generally in their country, and treated to the best that they could give me . . . they have often escorted me through their enemies' country at some hazard to their own lives . . . no Indian ever betrayed me, struck me a blow, or stole from me [any] of my property that I am aware of."

Catlin opened his Wild West Show in London, England, where he was joined by a group of Iowa, part of the Chippewa tribe. He described them as "a kind and hospitable people."

In an effort to improve his situation, Catlin decided to take the Wild West Show to Paris, France. French King Louis Philippe had purchased a copy of the *Indian Portfolio.* The king enthusiastically supported Catlin's idea of bringing the show to Paris and met with the artist at the royal palace in the city. In June 1845, the Wild West Show opened to enormous audiences. But it was quickly overtaken by tragedy when another one of the Iowa Indians died. The Iowas were already tired of Europe and wanted to go home to America. They decided it was time to leave.

No sooner had the Iowas departed than a more personal tragedy struck Catlin. Clara developed pneumonia, a serious lung illness, and died on July 28, 1845. She was only thirty-seven years old. "Her feeble form wasted away," Catlin wrote, and the loss was almost more than he could handle. He had been devoted to Clara, who had supported him throughout his career. He had left her alone for many months, while he had traveled among the Indian tribes of the West. Then Clara had come to England because George wanted her there. Hoping eventually to return to Albany, she kept seeing her voyage home postponed when George found additional reasons to stay in Europe. Now she would never see her home again.

Catlin's Declining Fortunes

With Clara's death, George became a single parent to four small children. He had to find a way to support them. When interest in his Wild West Show declined in Paris, he took the show to Belgium. But it was not successful there. Fortunately, King Louis Philippe came to Catlin's rescue and asked him to return to France to paint a group of pictures. This project helped the artist support his children. While he painted in his studio, Catlin's son, George, was his constant companion. "My dear little namesake, George, and my only boy, . . . adopted my painting room as his constant play-house."

Meanwhile, Catlin was writing letters to Washington, D.C., pleading with Congress to purchase his Indian Gallery. But once again, his request was turned down. However, this disappointment seemed small by comparison to the sudden loss of Catlin's son. George died of typhoid fever in summer 1846. Clara had been buried in Albany, and the little boy's body was also sent back New York, "as a lovely flower," Catlin wrote, "to be planted by the grave of his mother. Two idols of my heart had thus vanished . . . leaving my breast with a healing and a fresh wound, to be opened and bleeding together."

While he was devastated by George's death, Catlin had to keep painting to support his other three children. Fortunately, King Louis Philippe gave him another project—painting a series of pictures about the seventeenth-century French explorer Sieur de La Salle. But Catlin was never paid for the work. In 1848, a revolution occurred in Paris, and the king was driven from the throne. Amid the violence of the revolution, Catlin and his three children were lucky to escape the city and return to London.

Although Catlin received some work painting pictures, he earned very little money. He was unable to pay his debts and was eventually thrown into debtor's prison. At this point, Clara's brother, Dudley, a wealthy businessman, received information about Catlin's situation. He hurried to London and took the artist's three daughters back to the United States. Historians disagree about whether Catlin had asked Dudley to take the children or if Clara's family had decided to take this action themselves because they felt that Catlin was an unfit parent.

Soon afterward, Catlin left London and went back to Paris. At this point, one of the people to whom he owed money agreed to help him. Joseph Harrison, a wealthy locomotive manufacturer, took over the Indian Gallery and paid most of Catlin's debts. Harrison sent the Indian Gallery to his home in Philadelphia.

After so many dreams about bringing the culture of America's Indians to the world's audiences, Catlin now seemed to be left with nothing.

In 1870, George Catlin returned to the United States from Europe to exhibit his pictures.

CHAPTER SIX

Last Adventures

> . . . a people who live and keep what is their own
> without lock and key . . . And oh! How I love a
> people who don't live for the love of money.
> —*George Catlin*

After losing his children and his paintings, George Catlin went back to Paris in 1853. He summed up his situation this way: "My occupation gone, and with no other means on earth than my hands and my brushes, and less than half a life, at best, before me . . . my thoughts turned towards . . . fortune, to know if there was anything yet in store for me."

At age fifty-seven, when many men were considered old, there was still plenty "in store" for George Catlin. "The loss of my dear Clara," he later wrote, "my little Boy George, and . . . my Indian Collection—drove me almost to despair, but I mustered courage yet to live—yet to love—and again to trust my luck in the wilderness."

Since he had little work, the artist spent his days at the Bibliotheque Imperial, a large library in Paris. There he met a man who showed him a map of the Crystal Mountains in Brazil and told Catlin that a fortune in gold was hidden in their ancient mines. Catlin decided that his next adventure lay in Brazil, looking for the mines and painting the South American Indians who lived in the region. With the little money he had left, in 1853 Catlin boarded a ship for Caracas, Venezuela, on the northern coast of South America.

From Caracas, Catlin joined a small group of men who headed into the rain forests of South America. Before reaching the Crystal Mountains, the other men turned back. They had battled insects, poisonous snakes, and damp, rainy weather before losing their way and giving up the search. But Catlin would not give up. He was no longer interested in the gold mines, though; Catlin intended to paint the Indians of the region.

Catlin met a former slave from Cuba named Caesar Bolla. Caesar carried his paints and canvases, while the two men covered thousands of miles across the Americas. For Catlin, it was almost like the 1830s, as he rapidly produced one Indian portrait after another. Their journey took them to the southern tip of South America, then up the Pacific Coast to San Francisco. Heading northward, they reached Alaska and the Aleutian Islands and then crossed into Siberia. Finally, Catlin and Caesar retraced their steps down the coastline and headed inland toward the Rocky Mountains.

Along the way, Catlin painted Native American tribes, including the Chinook, the Walla Walla, and the Nez Percé, as well as magnificent landscapes. Eventually, the two men reached Mexico, where Catlin sketched the Indians of the Yucatan Peninsula.

After this journey, Catlin made a brief trip back to Europe. Then he turned around and began another painting trip in South America. By the early 1860s, he had returned to Europe again and begun to put the finishing touches on his paintings. Catlin, nearly deaf by this time, worked out of a tiny studio in Brussels, Belgium. In 1868, he published a book on his South American travels titled *Last Rambles Amongst the Indians of the Rocky Mountains and the Andes.*

Meanwhile, he also had begun another enormous project. From his notes, Catlin had begun to reproduce all the paintings he had made during the 1830s. The artist hoped that the United States Congress still might agree to hang these paintings in a giant exhibition of Indian culture. He also wanted to regain his position as an admired painter. As he wrote his brother Francis, "I am hard at work on the drawings—and as you can imagine, am working for a *name*—for the name of *Catlin.*"

In 1870, when he was seventy-four years old, Catlin put on a show of his works in Brussels. Then he boarded a ship, bringing his reproductions to the United States. At the dock in New York, Catlin met his three daughters. "Another man might have gone home with his daughters," wrote Marjorie Catlin Roehm, "and lived in comfort, but not George Catlin! His work was not yet done."

Catlin had arranged for an exhibition of his cartoons at the Sommerville Gallery in New York City. But the exhibit was very poorly attended. By this time, Americans were not interested in the culture of the Native American tribes. The Indians were being driven off their lands in a deadly war that was designed to make room for thousands of settlers heading west. Most people regarded the Indians as savages who stood in the way of progress and should be confined to reservations.

Soon after the exhibit closed, however, Catlin received a message from an old friend. Joseph Henry had become the director of the Smithsonian Institution in

CREATING THE CARTOONS

Catlin called his reproductions "cartoons." One of them was titled *Fire in a Missouri Meadow*. It portrays a prairie, with smoke rising on the horizon and Indian horsemen in the foreground. Catlin painted this picture on heavy paper. First he brushed on the blue sky, and then he painted the dark smoke clouds over parts of the sky. The prairie was created with a yellow-brown color. Then Catlin painted in the grass and the Indian horsemen. Lastly, the artist added the red and orange flames of the brush fire.

Fire in a Missouri Meadow and a Party of Sioux Escaping from It, Upper Missouri. George Catlin, 1832

Washington, D.C. He invited Catlin to come to Washington and hang his cartoons in the Smithsonian Institution. Henry also gave Catlin a small place to live and work at the Institution.

But Catlin's stay at the Smithsonian Institution was short. During fall 1872, he became very sick. He left the Smithsonian Institution to live near his daughters and their uncle, Dudley Gregory, in Jersey City, New Jersey. He died there on December 23, 1872.

As part of his Wild West Show, Catlin included an exhibit of Indian clothing and family life. "The reader will therefore see, that we mutually suffer in
each other's estimation from the unfortunate ignorance, which distance has
chained us in; . . . that the historian who would record justly and correctly
the character and customs of a people, must go and live among them."

Legacy of George Catlin

George Catlin did not receive the fame and recognition that he had hoped to achieve during his lifetime. His dream that Congress might buy his paintings and establish a magnificent Indian museum never came true. Seven years after his death, however, the family of Joseph Harrison gave Catlin's pictures to the Smithsonian Institution. Many of the pictures had been damaged and were not fully restored until the twentieth century. But eventually, they were hung in the Smithsonian Institution.

Art experts later criticized Catlin's works. The artist had never received formal training. Although he was a master at capturing the personalities of the Indians whom he painted in his portraits, to the art experts his portrayal of the Indians' figures seemed unsophisticated and crude.

But Catlin's purpose had never been to create finished masterpieces. His goal was to capture a traditional way of life and preserve it before the culture of the Indians disappeared. Unlike most people, Catlin could see that the Native American civilizations were being destroyed by white men. He wanted to record the victims of this destruction and their lifeways, almost as a photographer might capture them today.

Only recently has Catlin's great accomplishment been fully appreciated. Although other artists followed him and painted the Plains Indians, Catlin produced the most complete record of their way of life. He was as much a reporter as an artist, creating for future generations an indelible picture of a noble people and their vanishing civilization.

As settlers moved west, they killed off the buffaloes, which the Indians relied on to survive. Here, the native people are heading off, past Buffalo Bull, the Pawnee warrior, who is trapped beneath a dying buffalo bull.

Opposite: In his portrait of Buffalo Bull and hundreds of other pictures, Catlin preserved for all time the nobility of the American Indian.

Catlin was fascinated to observe the skill of Indians at hunting buffaloes. This lithograph appeared in Catlin's book *North American Indian Portfolio: Hunting Scenes and Amusements of the Rocky Mountains and Prairies of America*, which was published in 1845.

Glossary

Cartoon—Name given by Catlin to his reproductions of his paintings.

Culture—Shared beliefs, values, and practices that characterize a racial, religious, national, or social group.

Exhibition—A public showing, as of works of art; also called an "exhibit."

Firewater—A term used by Native Americans to refer to alcohol.

Indian Gallery—The name for Catlin's collection of paintings of American Indians.

Indian Removal Act—A law passed by the U.S. Congress in 1830 that authorized payments to the Indians for their land east of the Mississippi, encouraging them to move west.

Miniature—A small pocket-sized painting that a person carried, which usually portrayed a loved one.

Pipestone Quarry—The location of a red stone used to make Indian peace pipes.

Portfolio—A collection of paintings printed in book form, usually used for presentation.

Reservation—Location where Indians were required to move after selling or being forced to give up their land to white settlers.

Sketchbook—A pad of paper used by artists to make sketches, which often were later turned into paintings.

Steamboat—A vessel powered by steam that turned a waterwheel, located on the side of the boat or in the stern.

Territory—A geographic area in the United States that is not included within any state. Also any area claimed by one person or a group of people.

Trail of Tears—Forced relocation in 1838 of the Cherokee and other Native American tribes from Georgia to the western United States, which resulted in the deaths of an estimated 4,000 native people.

Treaty—An agreement made by negotiation between two political groups, as between the state or federal government and a Native American tribe.

Wild West Show—An exhibit of American Indian portraits and items from their villages, as well as demonstrations by Indians.

Time Line

1796: George Catlin is born on July 26 in Wilkes-Barre, Pennsylvania.

1808: Catlin attends elementary school in Hopbottom, Pennsylvania.

1812–1815: Conflict between the United States and Great Britain, known as the War of 1812.

1817: Catlin attends law School in Litchfield, Connecticut.

1818: Catlin begins law practice in Wilkes-Barre.

1820: Catlin opens an artist's studio in Philadelphia.

1824: He paints a portrait of New York Governor De Witt Clinton.

1828: Catlin marries Clara Gregory of Albany, New York.

1830: Catlin makes his first trip west to paint American Indians.

1831: Catlin returns west for his second painting trip.

1832: Traveling on the steamboat *Yellow Stone,* Catlin makes a third trip among the Indians.

1833: First exhibit of Catlin's works is held in Pittsburgh, Pennsylvania.

1834: Catlin travels west for a fourth trip to paint Indians.

1836: The artist makes his last trip west; paints Pipestone Quarry.

1837: Catlin opens an exhibit in New York City.

1838–1839: Catlin exhibits his work in Washington, Boston, and Philadelphia; he tries unsuccessfully to sell paintings to the U.S. government; and he travels to Europe to open his Wild West Show.

1841: He publishes a book, *Letters and Notes on the Manners, Customs, and Conditions of the North American Indians.*

1845: He publishes another book, *North American Indian Portfolio.* His wife, Clara Catlin, dies.

1846: His son, George Catlin, dies.

1848–1852: Catlin's debts increase; he sells the Indian Gallery to Joseph Harrison.

1853–1855: Catlin makes two trips to South America to paint Indians. He travels to Alaska and Mexico.

1860s: Catlin creates reproductions of his paintings of North American Indians.

1870: Catlin returns to the United States and exhibits the reproductions and other paintings.

1872: Catlin dies on December 23 in Jersey City, New Jersey.

Further Research

ABOUT HIS LIFE

Haverstock, Mary. *Indian Gallery: The Story of George Catlin.* New York: Four Winds, 1973.

Plain, Nancy. *George Catlin: The Man Who Painted Indians.* New York: Benchmark, 1997.

Rockwell, Anne. *Paintbrush and Peacepipe: The Story of George Catlin.* New York: Atheneum, 1971.

ABOUT HIS PAINTINGS

www.artcyclopedia.com/artists/catlin_george.html

Virtual tours of paintings held by museums and galleries, including the Fine Arts Museums of San Francisco, the Metropolitan Museum of Art, the National Gallery of Art, and the Smithsonian American Art Museum.

www.Catlinclassroom.si.edu/

An online exhibit from the Smithsonian Institute featuring paintings, historical documents, and commentary from contemporary experts on American Indian life and culture.

www.nga.gov/kids/catlin/catlin1.html

The National Gallery of Art's educational site for kids.

ABOUT THE PERIOD

Bial, Raymond. *The Iroquois.* Tarrytown, NY: Benchmark, 1998.

Calvert, Patricia. *The American Frontier.* New York: Atheneum, 1997.

Cornelissen, Cornelia. *Soft Rain: A Story of the Cherokee Trail of Tears.* New York: Delacorte, 1998.

Rice, Earle. *Life Among the Great Plains Indians.* Farmington Hills, MI: Lucent, 1998.

Worth, Richard. *Westward Expansion and Manifest Destiny in American History.* Englewood Cliffs, NJ: Enslow, 2006.

Bibliography

Catlin, George. *Letters and Notes on the Manners, Customs, and Conditions of the North American Indians.* 1841. New York: Clarkson Potter, 1975.

McCracken, Harold. *George Catlin and the Old Frontier.* New York: Dial, 1959.

Roehm, Marjorie Catlin. *The Letters of George Catlin and His Family.* Berkeley: University of California Press, 1966.

Samuels, Peggy, et al. *Techniques of the Artists of the American West.* Secaucus, NJ: Wellfleet, 1990.

Sufrin, Mark. *George Catlin: Painter of the Indian West.* New York: Atheneum, 1991.

SOURCE NOTE

Letters and Notes on the Manners, Customs, and Conditions of the North American Indians is the source for Catlin's descriptions of his encounters with Native American peoples, places, and customs. In addition to the printed version listed above, this volume is available online at www.xmission.com/~drudy/mtman/html/catlin/.

Index

ABOUT THE AUTHOR

Richard Worth, a Connecticut-based writer, is the author of more than fifty books for young adults. These include biographies, histories, books on current events, and family living. He is a collector of American Impressionist paintings by Connecticut artists from the Old Lyme School. His interest in George Catlin grew out of books that he has written on the Apache Indians and America's Manifest Destiny.

PHOTO CREDITS

The photographs in this book are used by permission and through the courtesy of:

Art Resource, NY: Smithsonian American Art Museum, Washington, DC, 2, 12, 14, 15, 19 (top), 30, 32 (top), 35, 36, 38, 40, 41, 44, 45, 47, 51, 54, 58 (top right), 58 (top left), 58 (lower right), 58 (lower left), 59 (top right), 59 (top left), 59 (lower right), 59 (lower left), 70, 71, 72. *The New York Public Library:* Rare Books Division, Astor, Lenox and Tilden Foundations, 6, 34, 49, 56; Print Collection, Miriam and Ira D. Wallach Division of Art, Prints and Photographs, Astor, Lenox, and Tilden Foundations, 29 (top). *Thomas Gilcrease Institute of American History and Art, Tulsa, Oklahoma,* 10. *Corbis:* Bettmann, 16; Philadelphia Museum of Art, 23. *Bridgeman Art Library,* Newark Museum, New Jersey, USA, 19 (lower). *Litchfield Historical Society,* 21. *Pennsylvania Academy of Fine Arts, Philadelphia,* Artist: Charles Wilson Peale, Title: *The Artist in His Museum,* 1822, Oil on canvas 103¾ x 79⅞ in. Acc. #1878.1.2. Gift of Mrs. Sarah Harrison (The Joseph Harrison Jr. Collection), 24. *Museum of Nebraska Art Collection Kearney, Nebraska:* Titian Ramsey Peale, *Buffalo Hunt on the River Platte,* 1873, oil, 25. *Cornell University Library Division of Rare Books and Manuscripts,* 26. *R.W. Norton Art Gallery, Shreveport, LA,* 29 (lower). *The State Historical Society of Missouri, Columbia,* 32 (lower). Chicago Historical Society, 62. *Virginia Museum of Fine Art, Richmond:* The Paul Mellon Collection, 64. *Fine Arts Museums of San Francisco:* Gift of Mr. and Mrs. John D. Rockefeller 3rd, Acc. #1979.7.24, 67. *Smithsonian Institute Archives:* Record Unit 95, #78-3843, 68.

Cover Photos: Smithsonian American Art Museum, Washington, DC, Art Resource, NY.

DATE DUE

WITHDRAWN

WITHDRAWN